The Chronnoisseur

Concentrate Journal

www.lulu.com

Cover Design: Todd M. Schilling Design
Interior Design: Todd M. Schilling Design
Editor: Justin Klein
ISBN: 978-1-329-99721-9

The purpose of this journal is to chronicle the consumption of cannabis for individuals who like to enjoy the different flavors, aromas, and methods of consumption available. I hope this book will encourage people to savor the variation between different strains as well as the variations between the same strains from different growers and regions. This journal will be a means for you to note the flavors, appearance, method of consumption, as well as the overall experience you like the best and least. Utilize this as a quick reference guide to determine whether you would like a future choice in product, and whether that product has unbeknownst to you already been consumed by you in the method of which you are currently about to try again; because, let's be honest, sometimes we forget.

Enjoy Responsibly!

How to Fill Out

In the dispensary section list the name and/or location from which you purchased your cannabis. This will allow you to differentiate between strains in different regions and from dispensary/growers in the same region. The date section can be used as a reference to see whether the characteristics of your concentrates, or even your palate, have changed over time.

Next it is important to list the strain name of the concentrate you are tasting. Check whether the strain is an indica, sativa, or both for hybrid. The $/g section is meant for you to note the difference in prices between regions, dispensaries, and strains.

The next few sections are meant to help in describing the concentrate prior to consumption. Utilize the blank bars and pie charts under each heading to shade in the level of each descriptor written. The blank description area of this section should be used to elaborate on everything that the shading can not fully express.

These next sections will be used to describe the consumption of the concentrate. Under the method section, circle whether you consumed the concentrate through a joint, waterpipe or dry pipe. Fill out the taste and smoke sections in the same manner as you did with the shading above. The blank description under this section should be utilized to elaborate on the type of method of consumption, as well as the characteristics of the taste and smoke.

The final section is to capture your overall impression of the concentrate. Rate your overall experience on a scale of 1 through 10 and circle yes or no depending on whether you would recommend this to a peer.

Under experience you can describe what type of affect the concentrate had on you and a story of something that may have occurred while under the influence of that particular strain, using that particular method.

The following page is an example of how to complete the pages of your journal.

Date 7/15

Dispensary (name/location) Chalice - San Bernardino, CA

Strain Blue Dream

indica ☐
sativa ☑

Price 35 $/g

Color
☐ Dark
☑ Light

Clarity
☐ Opaque
☑ Clear

Stability
☐ Solid
☑ Liquid

Density
Rock ☑ Tight
Loose ☑ Crumbly
Heavy ☐
Light ☐

Scent
Pine/Earthy
Citrus
Skunk/Cheese
Floral

Description Light amber/gold shatter. See through in light. Maintained the scent properties of its flower.

Taste
Floral / Citrus / Cheese / Nutty / Earthy / Spicy / Peppery / Fruity

Smoke
Heavy ☐ Full
Light ☐ Whispy

Description Green slyme mothership with quartz bucket swing. Clean burn, light airy smoke, floral with light citrus mix.

Overall 6 /10

Recommend Yes No

Experience lighter focusing high, recommend for daytime use.

Date _____

Dispensary (name/location) _____

Strain _____ indica ☐ Price _____ $/g
                                      sativa ☐

Color   **Clarity**   **Stability**   **Density**   **Scent**

☐ Dark   ☐ Opaque   ☐ Solid   Rock ☐ Tight   Heavy ☐ ☐ ☐ ☐

☐ Light   ☐ Clear   ☐ Liquid   Loose ☐ Crumbly   Light

                                                                   Pine/Earthy Citrus Skunk/Cheese Floral

Description _____
_____

Taste

Floral Citrus
Fruity   Cheese
Peppery   Nutty
    Spicy Earthy

Smoke

Heavy ☐ Full

Light   Whispy

Description _____
_____

Overall _____ /10 _____   Recommend   Yes / No

Experience _____
_____
_____

Date _____

Dispensary (name/location) _____

Strain _____ indica ☐ Price _____ $/g
                          sativa ☐

Color   **Clarity**   **Stability**   **Density**   **Scent**

☐ Dark   ☐ Opaque   ☐ Solid   Rock ☐ Tight   Heavy ☐ ☐ ☐ ☐

☐ Light   ☐ Clear   ☐ Liquid   Loose ☐ Crumbly Light

Pine/Earthy Citrus Skunk/Cheese Floral

Description _____

_____

Taste   **Smoke**

Floral Citrus   Heavy ☐ Full
Fruity   Cheese
Peppery   Nutty   Light   Whispy
  Spicy Earthy

Description _____

_____

Overall _____ /10 _____   Recommend   Yes / No

Experience _____

_____

_____

Date _____

Dispensary (name/location) _____

Strain _____ indica ☐ sativa ☐ Price _____ $/g

Color
☐ Dark
☐ Light

Clarity
☐ Opaque
☐ Clear

Stability
☐ Solid
☐ Liquid

Density
Rock ☐ Tight
Loose ☐ Crumbly

Scent
Heavy ☐
Light ☐ ☐ ☐ ☐
Pine/Earthy Citrus Skunk/Cheese Floral

Description
_____
_____

Taste
Floral Citrus Cheese Nutty Earthy Spicy Peppery Fruity

Smoke
Heavy ☐ Full
Light ☐ Whispy

Description
_____
_____

Overall _____ /10

Recommend _____ Yes / No

Experience
_____
_____
_____

Date _____

Dispensary (name/location) _____

Strain _____
indica ☐
sativa ☐
Price _____ $/g

Color
☐ Dark
☐ Light

Clarity
☐ Opaque
☐ Clear

Stability
☐ Solid
☐ Liquid

Density
Rock ☐ Tight
Loose ☐ Crumbly

Scent
Heavy ☐
Light ☐
☐
☐
☐

Pine/Earthy
Citrus
Skunk/Cheese
Floral

Description _____

_____

Taste

Floral
Citrus
Fruity
Cheese
Peppery
Nutty
Spicy
Earthy

Smoke
Heavy ☐ Full
Light ☐ Whispy

Description _____

_____

Overall _____ /10 _____

Recommend Yes / No

Experience _____

_____

_____

Date _____

Dispensary (name/location) _____

Strain _____ indica ☐ sativa ☐ Price _____ $/g

Color
☐ Dark
☐ Light

Clarity
☐ Opaque
☐ Clear

Stability
☐ Solid
☐ Liquid

Density
Rock ☐ Tight
Loose ☐ Crumbly

Scent
Heavy ☐
Light ☐
Pine/Earthy
☐ Citrus
☐ Skunk/Cheese
☐ Floral

Description
_____

Taste

Fruity Floral Citrus Cheese Nutty Earthy Spicy Peppery

Smoke
Heavy ☐ Full
Light ☐ Whispy

Description
_____
_____

Overall ____ /10 ____

Recommend   Yes / No

Experience
_____
_____

Date _____

Strain _____
indica ☐
sativa ☐
Price _____ $/g

Color
☐ Dark
☐ Light

Clarity
☐ Opaque
☐ Clear

Stability
☐ Solid
☐ Liquid

Density
Rock ☐ Tight
Loose ☐ Crumbly

Scent
Heavy ☐ ☐ ☐ ☐
Light
Pine/Earthy Citrus Skunk/Cheese Floral

Description _____

_____

Taste

Floral Citrus
Fruity   Cheese
Peppery   Nutty
Spicy Earthy

Smoke
Heavy ☐ Full
Light ☐ Whispy

Description _____

_____

Overall _____ /10 _____

Recommend   Yes / No

Experience _____

_____

_____

Dispensary (name/location)

Strain

indica ☐
sativa ☐

Price $/g

Color

☐ Dark

☐ Light

Clarity

☐ Opaque

☐ Clear

Stability

☐ Solid

☐ Liquid

Density

Rock ☐ Tight

Loose ☐ Crumbly

Scent

Heavy ☐ ☐ ☐ ☐

Light

Pine/Earthy *Citrus* *Skunk/Cheese* *Floral*

Description

Taste

Floral *Citrus*
Fruity   *Cheese*
Peppery   *Nutty*
Spicy *Earthy*

Smoke

Heavy ☐ Full

Light   Whispy

Description

Overall   /10

Recommend   Yes / No

Experience

Date _____

Strain _____ indica ☐ Price _____ $/g
                        sativa ☐

Color   **Clarity**   **Stability**   **Density**   **Scent**

☐ Dark   ☐ Opaque   ☐ Solid   Rock ☐ Tight   Heavy ☐   ☐   ☐   ☐

☐ Light   ☐ Clear   ☐ Liquid   Loose ☐ Crumbly Light

                                                                    Pine/Earthy Citrus Skunk/Cheese Floral

Description _____

_____

Taste   **Smoke**

Floral   Citrus   Heavy ☐ Full

Fruity   Cheese

Peppery   Nutty   Light ☐ Whispy

Spicy   Earthy

Description _____

_____

Overall _____ /10   **Recommend**   Yes / No

Experience _____

_____

_____

Date _____

Dispensary (name/location) _____

Strain _____ indica ☐ sativa ☐   **Price** _____ $/g

Color   **Clarity**   **Stability**   **Density**   **Scent**

☐ Dark   ☐ Opaque   ☐ Solid   Rock ☐ Tight   Heavy ☐   ☐   ☐   ☐

☐ Light   ☐ Clear   ☐ Liquid   Loose ☐ Crumbly   Light

Pine/Earthy   *Citrus*   *Skunk/Cheese*   *Floral*

Description
_____
_____

Taste

Floral Citrus
Fruity   Cheese
Peppery   Nutty
Spicy Earthy

Smoke

Heavy ☐ Full

Light   Whispy

Description
_____
_____

Overall _____ /10 _____   **Recommend**   Yes / No

Experience
_____
_____
_____

Date _____

Dispensary (name/location) _____

Strain _____ indica ☐ Price _____ $/g
                                            sativa ☐

Color   **Clarity**   **Stability**   **Density**   **Scent**

☐ Dark   ☐ Opaque   ☐ Solid   Rock ☐ Tight   Heavy ☐   ☐   ☐   ☐

☐ Light   ☐ Clear   ☐ Liquid   Loose ☐ Crumbly Light ☐ *Pine/Earthy* *Citrus* *Skunk/Cheese* *Floral*

Description _____

_____

                              Taste   **Smoke**

                         Floral   Citrus   Heavy ☐ Full
                      Fruity   Cheese
                                                 Light ☐ Whispy
                      Peppery   Nutty

                        Spicy   Earthy

Description _____

_____

Overall _____ /10 _____   **Recommend**   Yes / No

Experience _____

_____

_____

Date _____

Dispensary (name/location) _____

Strain _____ indica ☐ Price _____ $/g
                                 sativa ☐

Color   **Clarity**   **Stability**   **Density**   **Scent**

☐ Dark   ☐ Opaque   ☐ Solid   Rock ☐ Tight   Heavy ☐ ☐ ☐ ☐

☐ Light   ☐ Clear   ☐ Liquid   Loose ☐ Crumbly Light ☐ ☐ ☐ ☐
                                                                      Pine/Earthy Citrus Skunk/Cheese Floral

Description _____

_____

Taste   **Smoke**

Floral Citrus   Heavy ☐ Full
Fruity   Cheese
Peppery   Nutty   Light ☐ Whispy
  Spicy Earthy

Description _____

_____

Overall _____ /10 _____   Recommend   Yes / No

Experience _____

_____

_____

Dispensary (name/location) _____

Strain _____

indica ☐
sativa ☐

Price _____ $/g

Color
☐ Dark

☐ Light

Clarity
☐ Opaque

☐ Clear

Stability
☐ Solid

☐ Liquid

Density
Rock ☐ Tight

Loose ☐ Crumbly

Scent
Heavy ☐

Light ☐

☐ ☐ ☐

Pine/Earthy *Citrus* *Skunk/Cheese* *Floral*

Description _____

_____

Taste
Floral   Citrus

Fruity   Cheese

Peppery   Nutty

Spicy   Earthy

Smoke
Heavy ☐ Full

Light ☐ Whispy

Description _____

_____

Overall _____ /10 _____

Recommend   Yes / No

Experience _____

_____

_____

Date _____

Dispensary (name/location) _____

Strain _____ indica ☐ sativa ☐   **Price** _____ $/g

| **Color** | **Clarity** | **Stability** | **Density** | **Scent** |

Color
☐ Dark
☐ Light

Clarity
☐ Opaque
☐ Clear

Stability
☐ Solid
☐ Liquid

Density
Rock ☐ Tight
Loose ☐ Crumbly

Scent
Heavy ☐
Light ☐

Pine/Earthy   Citrus   Skunk/Cheese   Floral

Description
_____
_____

Taste

Floral   Citrus
Fruity   Cheese
Peppery   Nutty
Spicy   Earthy

Smoke
Heavy ☐ Full
Light ☐ Whispy

Description
_____

Overall _____ /10 _____   **Recommend** _____ Yes / No

Experience
_____
_____
_____

Dispensary (name/location)

Strain   indica ☐   Price $/g
                                          sativa ☐

Color   Clarity   Stability   Density   Scent

☐ Dark   ☐ Opaque   ☐ Solid   Rock ☐ Tight   Heavy ☐ ☐ ☐ ☐

☐ Light   ☐ Clear   ☐ Liquid   Loose ☐ Crumbly   Light

Pine/Earthy   Citrus   Skunk/Cheese   Floral

Description

                                        Taste   **Smoke**

                                  Floral   Citrus   Heavy ☐ Full

                              Fruity   Cheese

                                                          Light ☐ Whispy

                              Peppery   Nutty

                                  Spicy   Earthy

Description

Overall _____ /10 _____   Recommend   Yes / No

Experience

Dispensary (name/location)

Strain   indica ☐   Price $/g
                                sativa ☐

Color   **Clarity**   **Stability**   **Density**   **Scent**

☐ Dark   ☐ Opaque   ☐ Solid   Rock ☐ Tight   Heavy ☐ ☐ ☐ ☐

☐ Light   ☐ Clear   ☐ Liquid   Loose ☐ Crumbly   Light

Pine/Earthy   *Citrus*   *Skunk/Cheese*   *Floral*

Description

___

Taste   **Smoke**

Floral Citrus   Heavy ☐ Full

Fruity   Cheese

Peppery   Nutty   Light   Whispy

Spicy Earthy

Description

___

Overall   /10   Recommend   Yes / No

Experience

Date _____

Dispensary (name/location) _____

Strain _____ indica ☐ sativa ☐ **Price** _____ $/g

Color	**Clarity**	**Stability**	**Density**	**Scent**

Color
☐ Dark
☐ Light

Clarity
☐ Opaque
☐ Clear

Stability
☐ Solid
☐ Liquid

Density
Rock ☐ Tight
Loose ☐ Crumbly

Scent
Heavy ☐ ☐ ☐ ☐ Light
Pine/Earthy Citrus Skunk/Cheese Floral

Description _____

_____

Taste

Floral Citrus
Fruity   Cheese
Peppery   Nutty
Spicy Earthy

Smoke
Heavy ☐ Full
Light ☐ Whispy

Description _____

_____

Overall _____ /10 _____   **Recommend**   Yes / No

Experience _____

_____

_____

Date _____

Dispensary (name/location) _____

Strain _____   indica ☐   Price _____ $/g
                          sativa ☐

Color   **Clarity**   **Stability**   **Density**   **Scent**

☐ Dark   ☐ Opaque   ☐ Solid   Rock ☐ Tight   Heavy ☐ ☐ ☐ ☐

☐ Light   ☐ Clear   ☐ Liquid   Loose ☐ Crumbly   Light
                                                                        Pine/Earthy Citrus Skunk/Cheese Floral

Description
_____

_____

Taste   **Smoke**

Floral Citrus   Heavy ☐ Full
Fruity   Cheese
Peppery   Nutty   Light   Whispy
   Spicy Earthy

Description
_____
_____

Overall _____ /10 _____   Recommend _____ Yes / No

Experience
_____
_____

Dispensary (name/location) _____

Strain _____ indica ☐ **Price** _____ $/g
                                      sativa ☐

Color   **Clarity**   **Stability**   **Density**   **Scent**

☐ Dark   ☐ Opaque   ☐ Solid   Rock ☐ Tight   Heavy ☐ ☐ ☐ ☐

☐ Light   ☐ Clear   ☐ Liquid   Loose ☐ Crumbly Light

Pine/Earthy   Citrus   Skunk/Cheese   Floral

Description _____

_____

Taste   **Smoke**

Floral Citrus   Heavy ☐ Full
Fruity   Cheese
Peppery   Nutty   Light   Whispy
   Spicy Earthy

Description _____

_____

Overall _____ /10 _____   **Recommend**   Yes / No

Experience _____

_____

_____

Date _____

Dispensary (name/location) _____

Strain _____ indica ☐ Price _____ $/g
                        sativa ☐

Color   **Clarity**   **Stability**   **Density**   **Scent**

☐ Dark   ☐ Opaque   ☐ Solid   Rock ☐ Tight   Heavy ☐ ☐ ☐ ☐

☐ Light   ☐ Clear   ☐ Liquid   Loose ☐ Crumbly Light
                                                          Pine/Earthy Citrus Skunk/Cheese Floral

Description _____

_____

Taste   **Smoke**

Floral Citrus   Heavy ☐ Full
Fruity   Cheese
Peppery   Nutty   Light   Whispy
Spicy Earthy

Description _____

_____

Overall _____ /10 _____   **Recommend**   Yes / No

Experience _____

_____

_____

Date _____

Dispensary (name/location) _____

Strain _____   indica ☐   Price _____ $/g
                         sativa ☐

Color   **Clarity**   **Stability**   **Density**   **Scent**

☐ Dark   ☐ Opaque   ☐ Solid   Rock ☐ Tight   Heavy ☐ ☐ ☐ ☐

☐ Light   ☐ Clear   ☐ Liquid   Loose ☐ Crumbly Light

Pine/Earthy   Citrus   Skunk/Cheese   Floral

Description _____

Taste

Floral Citrus
Fruity   Cheese
Peppery   Nutty
  Spicy Earthy

Smoke

Heavy ☐ Full

Light ☐ Whispy

Description _____
_____

Overall _____ /10 _____   **Recommend**   Yes / No

Experience _____
_____
_____

Date _____

Dispensary (name/location) _____

Strain _____

indica ☐
sativa ☐

Price _____ $/g

Color
☐ Dark
☐ Light

Clarity
☐ Opaque
☐ Clear

Stability
☐ Solid
☐ Liquid

Density
Rock ☐ Tight
Loose ☐ Crumbly

Scent
Heavy ☐
Light ☐

Pine/Earthy

☐ Citrus

☐ Skunk/Cheese

☐ Floral

Description _____
_____

Taste

Floral Citrus
Fruity   Cheese
Peppery   Nutty
Spicy Earthy

Smoke
Heavy ☐ Full
Light ☐ Whispy

Description _____
_____

Overall _____ /10 _____

Recommend   Yes / No

Experience _____
_____
_____

Date _____

Dispensary (name/location) _____

Strain _____ indica ☐ sativa ☐   Price _____ $/g

Color   **Clarity**   **Stability**   **Density**   **Scent**

☐ Dark   ☐ Opaque   ☐ Solid   Rock ☐ Tight   Heavy ☐ ☐ ☐ ☐

☐ Light   ☐ Clear   ☐ Liquid   Loose ☐ Crumbly Light

Pine/Earthy   Citrus   Skunk/Cheese   Floral

Description _____

_____

Taste   **Smoke**

Floral Citrus   Heavy ☐ Full

Fruity   Cheese

Peppery   Nutty   Light ☐ Whispy

Spicy Earthy

Description _____

_____

Overall _____ /10 _____   Recommend   Yes / No

Experience _____

_____

_____

Date _____

Dispensary (name/location) _____

Strain _____ indica ☐ Price _____ $/g
                                     sativa ☐

Color   **Clarity**   **Stability**   **Density**   **Scent**

☐ Dark   ☐ Opaque   ☐ Solid   Rock ☐ Tight   Heavy ☐ ☐ ☐ ☐

☐ Light   ☐ Clear   ☐ Liquid   Loose ☐ Crumbly   Light ☐ ☐ ☐ ☐

                                                                      Pine/Earthy Citrus Skunk/Cheese Floral

Description _____

_____

_____

Taste   **Smoke**

Floral Citrus   Heavy ☐ Full
Fruity   Cheese
Peppery   Nutty   Light   Whispy
  Spicy Earthy

Description _____

_____

Overall _____ /10 _____   Recommend   Yes / No

Experience _____

_____

_____

Date _____

Dispensary (name/location) _____

Strain _____   indica ☐   Price _____ $/g
                                sativa ☐

Color   **Clarity**   **Stability**   **Density**   **Scent**

☐ Dark   ☐ Opaque   ☐ Solid   Rock ☐ Tight   Heavy ☐   ☐   ☐   ☐

☐ Light   ☐ Clear   ☐ Liquid   Loose ☐ Crumbly Light

                                                                        Pine/Earthy Citrus Skunk/Cheese Floral

Description _____

_____

                                    Taste   **Smoke**

                              Floral   Citrus   Heavy ☐ Full
                         Fruity   Cheese
                                                      Light ☐ Whispy
                         Peppery   Nutty

                              Spicy   Earthy

Description _____

_____

Overall _____ /10   **Recommend**   Yes / No

Experience _____

_____

_____

Date _____

Dispensary (name/location) _____

Strain _____   indica ☐   Price _____ $/g
                         sativa ☐

Color   **Clarity**   **Stability**   **Density**   **Scent**
☐ Dark   ☐ Opaque   ☐ Solid   Rock ☐ Tight   Heavy ☐ ☐ ☐ ☐
☐ Light   ☐ Clear   ☐ Liquid   Loose ☐ Crumbly   Light ☐ ☐ ☐ ☐
                                                                                 Pine/Earthy Citrus Skunk/Cheese Floral

Description
_____

Taste   **Smoke**
Floral Citrus   Heavy ☐ Full
Fruity   Cheese
Peppery   Nutty   Light ☐ Whispy
Spicy Earthy

Description
_____
_____

Overall _____ /10 _____   **Recommend** Yes / No

Experience
_____
_____
_____

Date _____

Strain _____   indica ☐   Price _____ $/g
   sativa ☐

Color   **Clarity**   **Stability**   **Density**   **Scent**

☐ Dark   ☐ Opaque   ☐ Solid   Rock ☐ Tight   Heavy ☐ ☐ ☐ ☐

☐ Light   ☐ Clear   ☐ Liquid   Loose ☐ Crumbly   Light

Pine/Earthy   *Citrus*   *Skunk/Cheese*   *Floral*

Description _____

_____

Taste

Floral   Citrus
Fruity   Cheese
Peppery   Nutty
Spicy   Earthy

Smoke

Heavy ☐ Full

Light ☐ Whispy

Description _____

_____

Overall _____ /10 _____   Recommend   Yes / No

Experience _____

_____

_____

Date _____

Strain _____ indica ☐ Price _____ $/g
sativa ☐

Color   **Clarity**   **Stability**   **Density**   **Scent**

☐ Dark   ☐ Opaque   ☐ Solid   Rock ☐ Tight   Heavy ☐ ☐ ☐ ☐

☐ Light   ☐ Clear   ☐ Liquid   Loose ☐ Crumbly Light

Pine/Earthy *Citrus* *Skunk/Cheese* *Floral*

Description _____

_____

Taste   **Smoke**

Floral Citrus   Heavy ☐ Full

Fruity   Cheese

Peppery   Nutty   Light   Whispy

Spicy Earthy

Description _____

_____

Overall _____ /10 _____   **Recommend**   Yes / No

Experience _____

_____

_____

Date _____

Dispensary (name/location) _____

Strain _____ indica ☐ **Price** _____ $/g
                                  sativa ☐

Color   **Clarity**   **Stability**   **Density**   **Scent**

☐ Dark   ☐ Opaque   ☐ Solid   Rock ☐ Tight   Heavy ☐ ☐ ☐ ☐

☐ Light   ☐ Clear   ☐ Liquid   Loose ☐ Crumbly Light

Pine/Earthy   Citrus   Skunk/Cheese   Floral

Description _____

_____

Taste   **Smoke**

Floral Citrus   Heavy ☐ Full
Fruity   Cheese
Peppery   Nutty   Light ☐ Whispy
   Spicy Earthy

Description _____

_____

Overall _____ /10 _____   **Recommend**   Yes / No

Experience _____

_____

_____

Date _____

Dispensary (name/location) _____

Strain _____

indica ☐
sativa ☐

Price _____ $/g

Color
☐ Dark
☐ Light

Clarity
☐ Opaque
☐ Clear

Stability
☐ Solid
☐ Liquid

Density
Rock ☐ Tight
Loose ☐ Crumbly

Scent
Heavy ☐
Light ☐

Pine/Earthy
Citrus
Skunk/Cheese
Floral

Description _____

Taste

Fruity
Floral
Citrus
Cheese
Nutty
Earthy
Spicy
Peppery

Smoke
Heavy ☐ Full
Light ☐ Whispy

Description _____

Overall _____ /10 _____

Recommend _____ Yes / No

Experience _____

Dispensary (name/location) _____

Strain _____ indica ☐ Price _____ $/g
                             sativa ☐

Color   Clarity   Stability   Density   Scent

☐ Dark   ☐ Opaque   ☐ Solid   Rock ☐ Tight   Heavy ☐ ☐ ☐ ☐

☐ Light   ☐ Clear   ☐ Liquid   Loose ☐ Crumbly Light ☐ ☐ ☐ ☐

Pine/Earthy *Citrus* *Skunk/Cheese* *Floral*

Description _____

_____

Taste   Smoke

Floral Citrus   Heavy ☐ Full

Fruity   Cheese

Peppery   Nutty   Light ☐ Whispy

Spicy Earthy

Description _____

_____

Overall _____ /10 _____   Recommend   Yes / No

Experience _____

_____

_____

Date _____

Dispensary (name/location) _____

Strain _____ indica ☐ sativa ☐   **Price** _____ $/g

Color
☐ Dark
☐ Light

Clarity
☐ Opaque
☐ Clear

Stability
☐ Solid
☐ Liquid

Density
Rock ☐ Tight
Loose ☐ Crumbly

Scent
Heavy ☐ ☐ ☐ ☐
Light

Pine/Earthy Citrus Skunk/Cheese Floral

Description _____
_____

Taste

Floral Citrus
Fruity   Cheese
Peppery   Nutty
Spicy Earthy

Smoke
Heavy ☐ Full
Light   Whispy

Description _____
_____

Overall _____ /10 _____   **Recommend**   Yes / No

Experience _____
_____
_____

Date _____

Strain _____   indica ☐   Price _____ $/g
                          sativa ☐

Color   **Clarity**   **Stability**   **Density**   **Scent**

☐ Dark   ☐ Opaque   ☐ Solid   Rock ☐ Tight   Heavy ☐ ☐ ☐ ☐

☐ Light   ☐ Clear   ☐ Liquid   Loose ☐ Crumbly Light

Pine/Earthy   *Citrus*   *Skunk/Cheese*   *Floral*

Description _____

Taste

Floral Citrus
Fruity   Cheese
Peppery   Nutty
   Spicy Earthy

Smoke

Heavy ☐ Full

Light ☐ Whispy

Description _____
_____

Overall _____ /10 _____   **Recommend**   Yes / No

Experience _____
_____
_____
_____

Date _____

Dispensary (name/location) _____

Strain _____ indica ☐ sativa ☐ **Price** _____ $/g

Color
☐ Dark
☐ Light

Clarity
☐ Opaque
☐ Clear

Stability
☐ Solid
☐ Liquid

Density
Rock ☐ Tight
Loose ☐ Crumbly

Scent
Heavy ☐ Light
☐ Pine/Earthy
☐ Citrus
☐ Skunk/Cheese
☐ Floral

Description _____

_____

Taste

Floral · Citrus · Cheese · Nutty · Earthy · Spicy · Peppery · Fruity

Smoke
Heavy ☐ Full
Light ☐ Whispy

Description _____

_____

Overall _____ /10 _____   **Recommend** Yes / No

Experience _____

_____

_____

Dispensary (name/location)

Strain

indica ☐
sativa ☐

Price $/g

Color
☐ Dark
☐ Light

Clarity
☐ Opaque
☐ Clear

Stability
☐ Solid
☐ Liquid

Density
Rock ☐ Tight
Loose ☐ Crumbly

Scent
Heavy ☐
Light ☐

☐ ☐ ☐

Pine/Earthy   Citrus   Skunk/Cheese   Floral

Description

Taste

Floral · Citrus · Cheese · Nutty · Earthy · Spicy · Peppery · Fruity

Smoke
Heavy ☐ Full
Light ☐ Whispy

Description

Overall   /10

Recommend   Yes / No

Experience

I hope you enjoyed "working" your way through this journal.

May this be an addition to many volumes of

The Chronnoisseur

in your collection!